GREEK MYTHOLOGY

ZEUS,
King of the Gods

BY JOANNA BLAIR

Enslow PUBLISHING

Please visit our website, www.enslow.com. For a free color catalog of all our high-quality books, call toll free 1-800-398-2504 or fax 1-877-980-4454.

Cataloging-in-Publication Data
Names: Blair, Joanna.
Title: Zeus, king of the gods / Joanna Blair.
Description: Buffalo, NY : Enslow Publishing, 2027. | Series: Greek mythology | Includes glossary and index.
Identifiers: ISBN 9781978550988 (pbk.) | ISBN 9781978550995 (library bound) | ISBN 9781978551008 (ebook)
Subjects: LCSH: Zeus (Greek deity)--Juvenile literature. | Gods, Greek--Juvenile literature. | Mythology, Greek--Juvenile literature.
Classification: LCC BL820.J8 B535 2027 | DDC 292.2113--dc23

Published in 2027 by
Enslow Publishing
2544 Clinton Street
Buffalo, NY 14224

Portions of this work were originally authored by Christine Ha and published as *Zeus*. All new material in this edition was authored by Joanna Blair.

Cover Designer: Joshua Olson
Interior Designer: Joshua Olson
Editor: Claire Vanden Branden

Photo Credits: Cover, p. 1 Solarisys/Shutterstock.com; pp. 4–5 SandraSWC/Shutterstock.com; pp. 6–7 Lucian Milasan/Shutterstock.com; p. 8 Sergey Goryachev/Shutterstock.com; p. 9 tan_tan/Shutterstock.com; pp. 10–11 Clara/Shutterstock.com; pp. 12–13 Drawlab19/Shutterstock.com; pp. 14–15, 18 delcarmat/Shutterstock.com; pp. 16–17 Tugrul Canakci/Shutterstock.com; pp. 19, 29 Morphart Creation/Shutterstock.com; pp. 20–21 Rawpixel.com/Shutterstock.com; pp. 22–23 Ed Goodacre/Shutterstock.com; pp. 24–25 isparklinglife/Shutterstock.com; p. 26 Asgold/Shutterstock.com; p. 27 blackboard1965/Shutterstock.com.

Printed in China

CPSIA compliance information: Batch #QS27ENS: For further information contact Enslow Publishing, at 1-800-398-2504.

TABLE OF CONTENTS

CHAPTER 1

GOD OF THUNDER

Zeus was the god of thunder and lightning. He had power over weather. He could control storms, rain, and wind.

Zeus had a golden eagle. It carried messages for him.

Zeus ruled both gods and humans. He watched over them from Mount Olympus. Zeus **punished** evil people. But he rewarded good deeds.

Prometheus stole some of Zeus's lightning. So, Zeus made an eagle attack him.

HARSH PUNISHMENTS

Zeus could be **harsh** when he punished people. One man was doomed to roll a huge rock up a hill forever. Another was tied to a flaming wheel.

Zeus was married to the goddess Hera. However, he had many lovers. Some were goddesses. Others were humans. Zeus had many children with them.

Once, Zeus fell in love with Leto. They had two children together.

Zeus could turn himself into an animal. He sometimes came to Earth as a swan or a bull.

Some of Zeus's children grew up to be heroes. Others were gods or goddesses.

CHAPTER 2

THE FIGHT TO RULE

According to legend, Zeus was the son of Cronus. Cronus was a **Titan**. He ruled the world. But he was told his children would **overthrow** him.

Legends say Cronus ruled over harvests. Farmers prayed to him for help growing crops.

Cronus tried to swallow Zeus. But Zeus's mother gave Cronus a rock to swallow instead.

Cronus wanted to stay in power. So, he decided to swallow his children. Only Zeus escaped. When Zeus grew up, he made Cronus cough up his siblings. Together, they went to war against Cronus.

The gods Hades and Poseidon were Zeus's brothers.

The war lasted 10 years. Finally, Zeus took the throne from his father. He became the new ruler.

CHALLENGING ZEUS

Once, some gods tried to overthrow Zeus. They stole his lightning and tied him up. But he escaped and punished them. They never challenged him again.

Together, Zeus and his siblings defeated Cronus.

CHAPTER 3

FAMOUS MYTHS

Once, a group of giants tried to overthrow the gods. But Zeus and the other gods fought back. The gods won the battle.

The giants who fought against the Greek gods were children of the goddess Gaia.

Zeus asked another god to create the first woman. Zeus gave the woman a box. He told her not to open it. It was full of evil. But she opened the box. So, the evil went out into the world.

In Greek myths, the first woman's name was Pandora.

Four horses who could never die pulled Zeus's chariot.

WIND GODS

In addition to Zeus, the Greeks worshipped four wind gods. Some stories say these gods turned into horses to pull Zeus's **chariot**.

Humans were not allowed on Mount Olympus.

According to legend, 12 main Greek gods lived on Mount Olympus.

One of Zeus's most famous children was Hercules. Hercules was half human. But he became a great hero. So, he was able to join Zeus and the other gods on Mount Olympus.

CHAPTER 4

HONORING ZEUS

Zeus was popular all over Greece. Many homes had **altars** to him. People believed Zeus would protect their families.

Zeus is often shown as a strong man with a long beard.

A temple of Zeus still stands today in Athens, Greece.

The Greeks also built temples for Zeus. The temples stood on hills or mountains. People visited them to pray for rain.

One temple had a huge statue of Zeus. It stood about 40 feet (12 m) tall.

One major temple was in Olympia. This city **hosted** the Olympic Games. This **festival** was held to honor Zeus. It featured many sports.

Discus throwing was part of the Olympics. A discus is a heavy metal plate.

Olive trees grew near Zeus's temple in Olympia. Their leaves were symbols of victory and peace.

At the Olympics, winners were given crowns of olive leaves.

OLYMPIC GAMES

The Olympic Games took place every four years. People came from all over Greece to watch and **compete**. Events included races and wrestling.

TEST YOUR KNOWLEDGE

Take this quiz to test your knowledge.

1. Write a few sentences explaining how Zeus came to power.

2. Do you think Zeus was a good ruler? Why or why not?

3. What kind of being was Cronus, Zeus's father?

   A. a human
   B. a hero
   C. a Titan

4. Why might temples for Zeus be built on mountains?

   A. The temples could be near the sky and weather.
   B. The temples could be too high to visit.
   C. Only people on mountains worshipped Zeus.

5. What does **rewarded** mean in this book?

*Zeus punished evil people. But he **rewarded** good deeds.*

A. thanked people for doing things
B. stopped people from doing things
C. hurt or made fun of people

6. What does **popular** mean in this book?

*Zeus was **popular** all over Greece. Many homes had altars to him.*

A. not very well-known
B. liked by many people
C. very hard to find

Answers can be found on page 32.

GLOSSARY

altars
Tables used for prayers, offerings, or other religious actions.

chariot
A two-wheeled cart pulled by horses or other animals.

compete
To try to beat others in a game or event.

festival
A day or time of celebration, often based on a religion.

harsh
Very hard or mean, especially in a way that is unfair.

hosted
Planned an event or provided the space where it happened.

overthrow
To remove someone from power.

punished
Forced someone to do something hard or painful after doing something wrong.

Titan
A type of huge, powerful giant. In Greek mythology, Titans ruled the earth before the gods did.

FOR MORE INFORMATION

BOOKS

Buckey, A. W. *Greek Mythology Gods*. San Diego, CA: BrightPoint Press, 2022.

Hudak, Heather C. *Zeus*. Minneapolis, MN: Abdo Publishing, 2022.

WEBSITES

Britannica Kids: Zeus
kids.britannica.com/kids/article/Zeus/353952
Read more about Zeus.

National Geographic: The Gods and Goddesses of Ancient Greece!
natgeokids.com/nz/discover/history/greece/greek-gods
Learn more about Greek gods and goddesses.

Publisher's note to educators and parents: Our editors have carefully reviewed these websites to ensure that they are suitable for students. Many websites change frequently, however, and we cannot guarantee that a site's future contents will continue to meet our high standards of quality and educational value. Be advised that students should be closely supervised whenever they access the internet.

INDEX

Answer Key:
1. Answers will vary; 2. Answers will vary; 3. C; 4. A; 5. A; 6. B